KV-192-017

ASIA

Go Exploring! Continents and Oceans

By Steffi Cavell-Clarke

©2017
Book Life
King's Lynn
Norfolk PE30 4LS

ISBN: 978-1-78637-050-1

All rights reserved
Printed in Malaysia

Written by:
Steffi Cavell-Clarke

Edited by:
Grace Jones

Designed by:
Natalie Carr

A catalogue record for this book
is available from the British Library.

ASIA

CONTENTS

*Words in **red** can be found in the glossary on page 23.*

WHAT IS A CONTINENT?

A continent is a very large area of land that covers part of the earth's surface. There are seven continents in total. There are also five oceans that surround the seven continents.

ARCTIC OCEAN

NORTH AMERICA

EUROPE

ASIA

ATLANTIC OCEAN

AFRICA

SOUTH AMERICA

EQUATOR

INDIAN OCEAN

AUSTRALIA

PACIFIC OCEAN

SOUTHERN OCEAN

ANTARCTICA

The seven continents are home to the earth's **population**. Each continent has many different types of weather, landscape and wildlife. Let's go exploring!

WHERE IS ASIA?

Asia is **located** to the north of the **equator**. It is to the east of Europe and to the north-east of Africa. It is connected to Europe and Africa by land while the rest of the continent is surrounded by oceans and seas.

Arctic Ocean

Asia

Indian Ocean

China

Asia is the largest continent in the world. It also includes many islands. Islands are areas of land that are completely surrounded by water. Japan, in the east of Asia, is made up of thousands of islands.

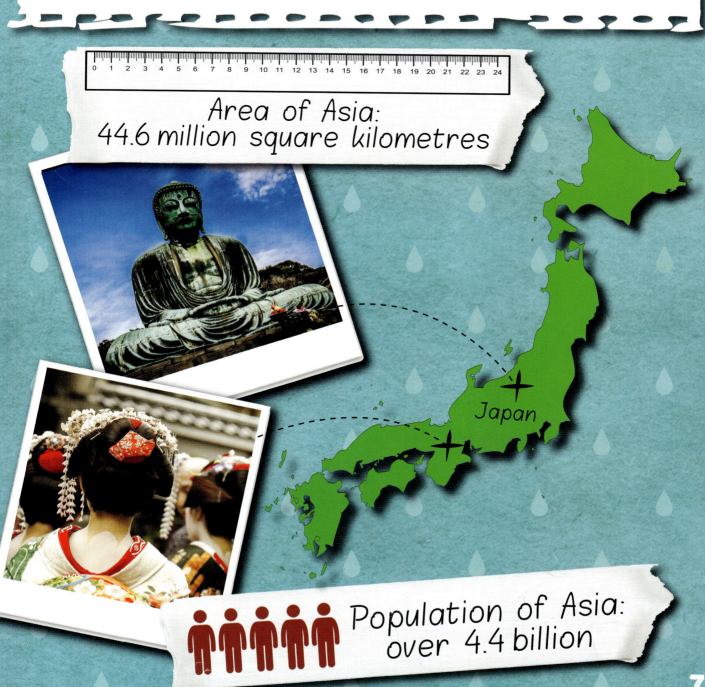

Area of Asia:
44.6 million square kilometres

Japan

Population of Asia:
over 4.4 billion

OCEANS

A sea is an extremely large area of salt water. The biggest seas in the world are called oceans. Just like countries, seas and oceans have different names.

Arctic Ocean

North America

Europe

Asia

Atlantic Ocean

Africa

Pacific Ocean

South America

Indian Ocean

Australi

Southern Ocean

Asia is mostly surrounded by the Pacific, Arctic and Indian Oceans.

FACT FILE

Pacific Ocean:
Area: 31% of the Earth's surface
Average Depth: 4,280 metres

Arctic Ocean:
Area: 2.8% of the Earth's surface
Average Depth: 1,038 metres

Indian Ocean:
Area: 13% of Earth's surface
Average Depth: 3,890 metres

Depth is how deep the water is.

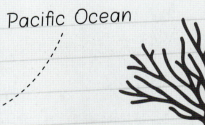

Arctic Ocean

Pacific Ocean

Indian Ocean

COUNTRIES

There are 50 countries in Asia. The largest countries are Russia and China.

Turkey

Turkmenistan

Uzbekistan

Russia

Azerbaijan

Tajikistan

Syria

Kazakhstan

Mongolia

North Korea

Kyrgyzstan

China

Japan

South Korea

Iran

Afghanistan

Pakistan

Bhutan

Myanmar

Jordan

India

Laos

Saudi Arabia

Oman

Vietnam

Iraq

United Arab Emirates

Philippines

Qatar

Yemen

Bangladesh

Sri Lanka

Cambodia

Indonesia

Malaysia

Thailand

Nepal

FACT FILE

Largest Country	Russia	Largest country in the world
Most Populated Country	China	Over 1.3 billion
Famous Landmark	The Great Wall of China	13,170 miles long
Highest Peak	Mount Everest, Himalayas	8,848 metres high
Largest Mammal	Asian Elephant	2.7 metres high

WEATHER

The **climate** in Asia changes across the continent. The continent has an icy and cold climate in the Arctic and a hot and **tropical** climate in the south.

The north of Russia is extremely cold; temperatures often fall below -20ºC.

Some areas of Asia have dry seasons and rainy seasons. In the dry season, there is very little rain and the ground is very dry, but in the rainy season it rains almost every day. This is also called the monsoon season.

Storm clouds in China

Moonson Season

LANDSCAPE

There are many different types of landscape across the continent of Asia. There are large deserts, high mountains, **grasslands** and forests.

Desert

Forest

The world's highest mountain is located between Nepal and China in Asia. The highest peak is Mount Everest at a height of 8,848 metres which is located along a **mountain range** called the Himalayas.

Asia

The Himalayas

Mount Everest

Russia has the most forests in the world. A forest is a large area of land that is covered in trees and other types of plant. The largest forest, called the Taiga, stretches from the western areas of Russia to the Pacific Ocean.

Taiga

Ocean Trench

Sea Bed

Underneath the surface of the Pacific and Indian Oceans that surround Asia, there is an uneven and rocky landscape. The Pacific and Indian Oceans have deep **valleys** in the sea bed called trenches.

WILDLIFE

Asia is home to many different types of wildlife that can be found all over the continent.

Peacock

Elephant

Stork

Camel

Panda

Tiger

Orangutan

33 metres

Bengal tigers can reach up to 3.3 metres long.

The Bengal tiger is found in India, Bangladesh and in other warm areas of desert and grassland across Asia. Tigers are carnivores, which means that they eat other animals. They feed on other large mammals such as deer.

SETTLEMENTS

China and India have the highest populations in the world. Millions of people live in in big cities across the continent.

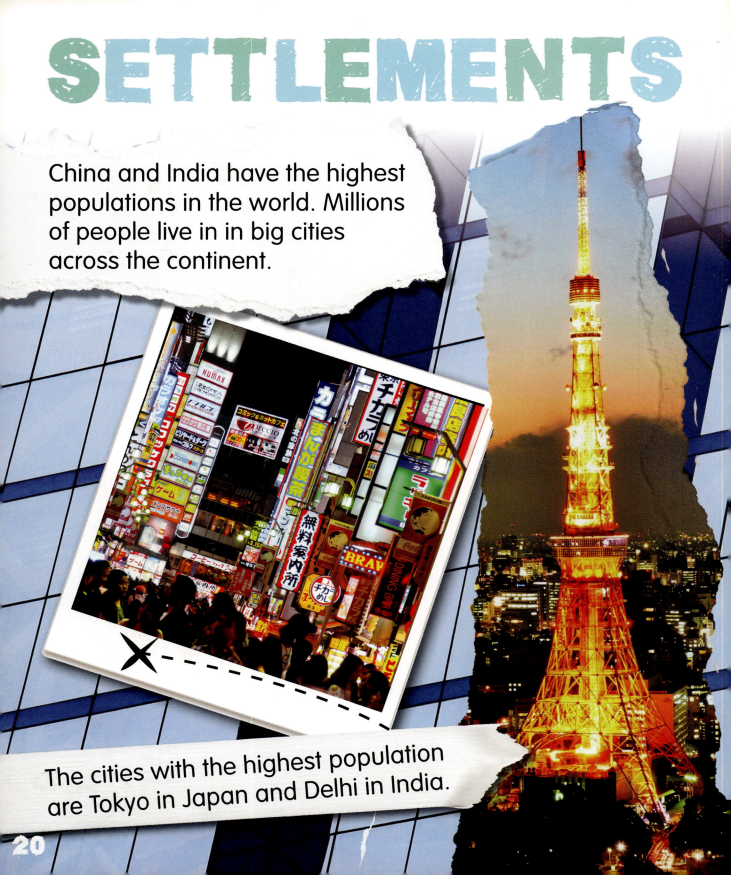

The cities with the highest population are Tokyo in Japan and Delhi in India.

There are also many people in Asia who live in the countryside. There are many farming villages where people often grow crops, such as rice and wheat. They can either eat their crops or sell them at the local market.

Wheat Plant

Market in Asia

THE ENVIRONMENT

There are many **endangered** animals in Asia. This means that a certain type of animal is close to becoming **extinct**. To help these animals, special areas of protected land have been made safe for the animals to live in.

Tigers are one of the best protected animals in Asia.

GLOSSARY

climate the average weather of an area

endangered when a type of animal is in danger of becoming extinct

equator imaginary line running around the middle of the earth

extinct a type of animal that is no longer living

grasslands large flat areas of grassy land

located where something can be found

mammal an animal that has warm blood, a backbone and usually has fur

mountain range a group of connected mountains

population number of people living in a place

tropical warm and wet areas near the equator

valleys long, narrow and deep dips in the land

INDEX

PHOTOCREDITS

Abbreviations: l–left, r–right, b–bottom, t–top, c–centre, m–middle.

Front Cover Background – 2t – Bule Sky Studio. 2br – Galyna Andrushko. 3tr – Viacheslav Lopatin. 3br – Efired. 5tl – Sean Pavone. 5tm – Praisaeng. 5tr – Viacheslav Lopatin. 5ml – Sean Pavone. 5mr – Efired. 6mr – Sean Pavone. 6–7 Background – Irtsya. 7ml – Kwan999. 7bl - tiffgraphic. 9b – ana_sky. 9m – 89studio. 9 Background – taviphoto. 12ml – Ozerov Alexander. 12mr – Kichigin. 13tl – Tim UR. 13ml - Daniel J. Rao. 13mr – Rudra Narayan Mitra. 13br – Rudra Narayan Mitra. 14 Background – pinyoj. 14tl – Barbara Barbour. 14tr – SIHASAKPRACHUM. 14bl – Emre Tarimcioglu. 14br – YURY TARANIK. 15 Background – number_two. 15bl – saiko3p. 15br – Daniel Prudek. 16 Background – avian. 16tl – Dmitry Strizhakov. 16 – Serg Zastavkin. 16 tr &bl – SeDmi. 17t – James Steidl. 17b - Jolanta Wojcicka. 18 Vectors - Muhammad Desta Laksana, Spreadthesign, Teguh Mujiono, sundatoon, Pushkin, Sign N Symbol Production, MusiggachartSMY. 20 Background – Lucy Liu. 20ml – erati Komson. 20mr – Hit1912. 21 Background – Incomible. 21ml – Zeljko Radojko. 21mr – polarbearstudio. 22ml – AppStock. 22mr – Martin Dallaire. Images are courtesy of Shutterstock.com. With thanks to Getty Images, Thinkstock Photo and iStockphoto.